W9-BDD-777

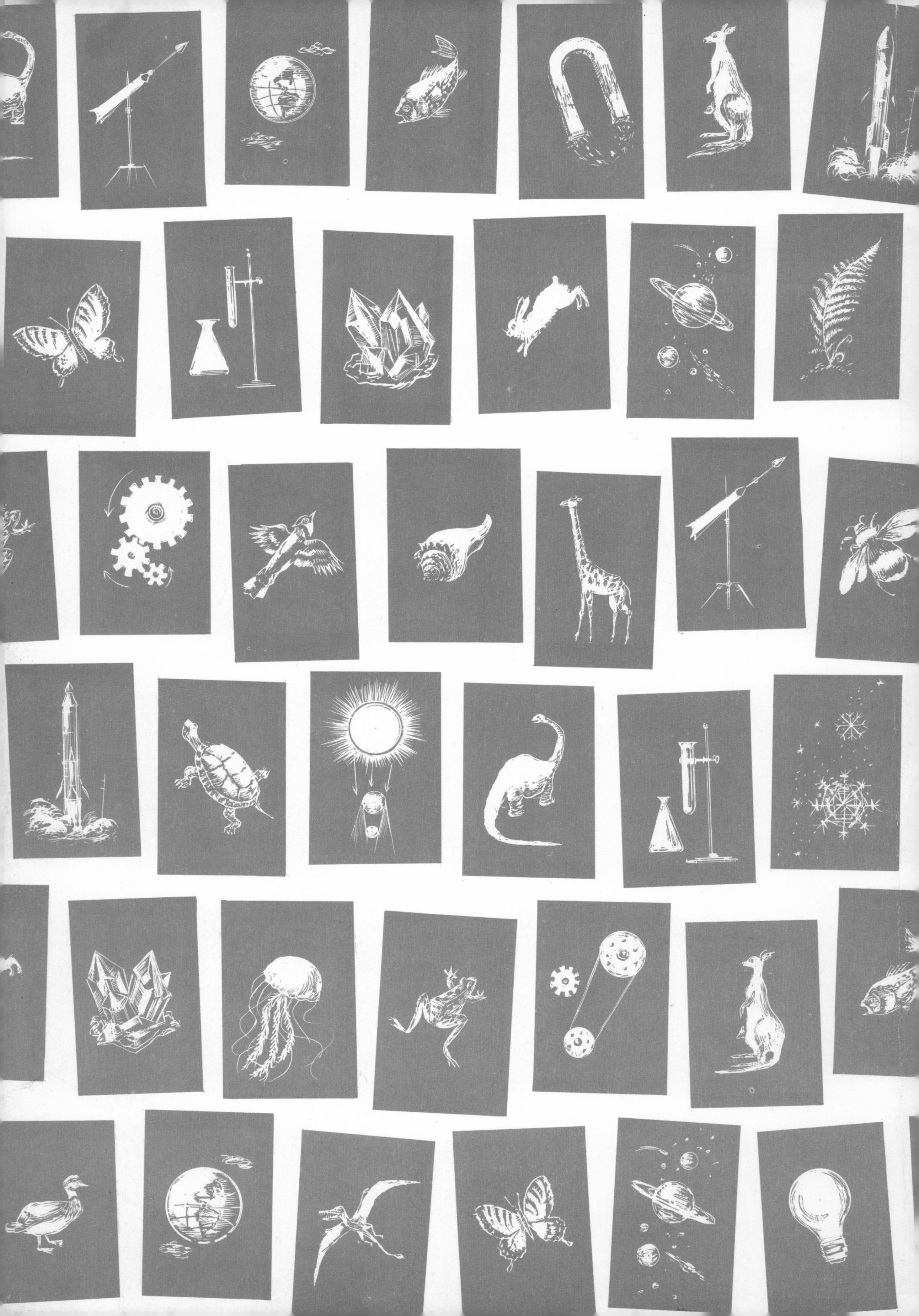

THE HOW AND WHY WONDER BOOK OF
WILD FLOWERS

Written by
GRACE F. FERGUSON, B.A.
Instructor, Brooklyn Botanic Garden

Illustrated by
CYNTHIA ILIFF KOEHLER
and ALVIN KOEHLER

Editorial Production:
DONALD D. WOLF

Edited under the supervision of
Dr. Paul E. Blackwood,
Washington, D. C.

Text and illustrations approved by
Oakes A. White, Brooklyn Children's Museum, Brooklyn, New York

GROSSET & DUNLAP • Publishers • NEW YORK

Introduction

Seldom has anyone walked in a park, through a forest, along a pasture's edge or on a mountain slope in spring without wondering about the name of some flower growing there.

Recognizing the flower is a part of enjoying it, but there is usually greater satisfaction in knowing some of the other important things about a plant and its surroundings — for example, how its flower differs from flowers on other plants; how its fruit develops; how its seeds are scattered; where it grows; what other plants usually grow near it; and how it is useful or harmful. These are the kinds of observations that really help one to interpret the world of plants.

The How and Why Wonder Book of Wild Flowers is a factual story of what botanists have learned about a very large group of plants — those uncultivated plants that bear flowers. It deals with the kind of information that will assist the curious reader in adding to his knowledge, and thereby help him to find increased pleasure in a vital area of wild life.

The book will be a most useful reference text at home and at school, whether it is used as part of a science study, as a hobby or as a reading adventure in natural history.

Paul E. Blackwood

Dr. Blackwood is a professional employee in the U. S. Office of Education. This book was edited by him in his private capacity and no official support or endorsement by the Office of Education is intended or should be inferred.

Library of Congress Catalog Card Number: 62-12790

Published simultaneously in Canada. Printed in the United States of America.

Contents

Study this illustration carefully; it is the "family tree" of the plant kingdom. It shows how plants developed from the earliest and most primitive forms to the most highly organized ones. At the same time, it shows how botanists have divided the plant kingdom. Some of these plants are smaller today than when they lived millions of years ago, but they still have the same general characteristics. All plants, scientists believe, developed from a very simple, one-celled organism called the PROTOPHYTA, which means "first plants." There are four main divisions in the plant kingdom: 1) THALOPHYTES; 2) BRYOPHYTES; 3) PTERIODOPHYTES; and 4) SPERMATOPHYTES. Spermatophytes are seed plants, the highest organisms in the plant kingdom and relative latecomers in the development of plants. The seed-bearers are divided into the GYMNOSPERMS or cone-bearers, and the ANGIOSPERMS or flowering plants.

FERN SHOWING SPORE SACS

Wild Flowers, Wanted and Unwanted

PUFFBALL MUSHROOM EJECTING A CLOUD OF SPORES

CATTAIL IN SEED

Cattail in bloom: the top part, producing only the stamens, falls off when the seed develops in the lower part, which produces only the pistils. You can see the tiny flowers under a magnifying glass.

What is a flowering plant?

All living things are divided into two main groups called the *plant kingdom* and the *animal kingdom*. Flowering plants are only one part of the whole plant kingdom. They are plants that, with a few exceptions, have roots, stems and leaves. At certain times they have flowers, fruits and seeds. The flowers are often very beautiful, but some plants have such small flowers that you would not notice them unless you looked very closely. When wild ginger is found in the woods, all that is seen at first are its leaves, but each plant has one little maroon flower growing just above the soil. It is sometimes half-buried by last year's leaves that fell from the trees. Grasses are plants with many very tiny flowers. They are interesting if you look at them through a magnifying glass. The cattail is one kind of grass with many small flowers packed so closely together that they form a solid brown spike.

Are there plants that have no flowers?

When you walk through fields or forests, there are many plants to be seen. Only some of them have flowers. Others have already finished flowering or will flower at a later time. But there are still other plants that never have any flowers at all. Among these are ferns, mosses and mushrooms. Ferns and mosses have green leaves, and mushrooms grow in many shapes and colors, such as red, yellow, brown and white. In place of the seeds of flowering plants, all these plants have spores from which new plants grow. The spores are very tiny. Hundreds of them together look like a little smear of dust. They grow enclosed in cases on the backs of fern leaves and on little stems arising from the tips of moss plants. In many mushrooms the spores grow under the umbrella-like cap. A puffball is a kind of mushroom that is likely to be found in the woods or fields. It is a round, white ball that turns brown and hard when the spores inside it are ready to come out. If a ripe brown puffball is pressed, some of the spores puff out like a little brown cloud of dust.

Weed or useful plant? For many people who have lawns, the dandelion is only a pest. For others who use dandelion leaves to make a vitamin-rich salad, or who use the flowers in making wine, or the plant's roots for the preparation of medical drugs, the dandelion is a very useful plant.

What makes a weed different from a useful plant?

Every kind of flowering plant has a place of origin somewhere in the world — a place where it grew before people began to carry plants from one place to another. Some plants grow wild only in a few places, while others grow wild over a large area. Some of them are very beautiful, and some can be used for food, clothing or other purposes. Some plants, whether or not they are pretty, become pests. Their seeds scatter far and wide into gardens and farms, where they grow so quickly that they crowd out the plants that the people want. These unwanted plants may spoil crops needed by the farmer, and they can make gardens unsightly places. A plant growing where someone doesn't want it to be is called a *weed.*

Dandelions growing in a lawn or flower bed are considered weeds. But some people purposely grow fields of dandelions in order to make wine from the juice of the flowers or to make salads from the leaves. To these people, the dandelions are certainly not weeds.

Therefore, the distinction between what we call "weeds" and "plants" has nothing to do with the flowers or plants themselves. The distinction is actually in the way people think of them. We call them "plants" if they are wanted and considered useful. We call them "weeds," however, if they are unwanted and considered useless.

What plants did European settlers find in America?

When the first European settlers came to America, they found some wild plants that were very much like the ones they had known in Europe. Wild strawberries, hepaticas, grapevines and lady-slipper orchids, as well as many others, grew in both places. But some of the American plants were unlike anything the settlers had seen before. Perhaps the most amazing plants to these people were the cacti, which grew only in America until people began taking them to other lands. Some other American plants were the dahlia, marigold, cranberry, tomato, potato and a tall grass called maize or Indian corn.

The American Indians had already discovered that some of these plants were good for food. For many years they had collected seeds of these plants and sown them in fields. They had learned that plants grow better if the soil is crumbled, allowing the roots to spread easily. They had also learned that if all other plants are pulled out, there will be more room for the crop. In other words, they had learned how to *cultivate* plants.

Where do cultivated varieties of plants come from?

Among plants of any one kind, there will be small differences of color or height or size of fruits and leaves, or of any other trait. If you have ever picked wild strawberries, you may have noticed that some berries are larger or sweeter than others. Sometimes this is due to the fact that one plant has plenty of room in which to grow, while another is being crowded by its neighbors. But even if wild strawberry plants are dug up and carefully grown under the best conditions, there will be differences among them. Some plants may have larger berries, and some may keep on producing berries after the others have stopped. If the seeds from only the best plants are sown, many of the new plants may be as good as the best of the first plants. Some may even be slightly better.

People actually have done this sort of selection of strawberry plants for perhaps hundreds of years. As a result, the *cultivated* varieties of strawberry plants that our farmers now grow produce berries that are much bigger than those of the wild plants. If as much time and effort had been used to select plants with *smaller* berries rather than larger ones, by now we might have had strawberries the size of pinheads. But, of course, no one is interested in such unprofitable selection.

The same process of selection has been used with many kinds of flowering plants. Wild zinnias growing in Mexico have small flowers. The flowers of cultivated varieties of zinnias come in all sizes up to six inches across.

The first settlers in America found some wild plants very similar to the ones they had known in Europe. Many plants, however, were quite different from European ones.

GRAPE

CRANBERRY

MAIZE

CACTUS

FLOWERS OF COASTS, MARSHES, LAKES AND RIVERS

Wild flowers grow almost everywhere on the earth, including streams, lakes and coastal regions. Some plants, such as the HALOPHYTES, live in marshes. Other plants, such as the HYDROPHYTES, are especially adapted for the extremely moist surroundings found in and about lakes, streams and swamps. The flowers on these two pages all belong to either of these two groups. Spatterdock, water lilies, bur reed and pickerelweed grow right out of the water. Mallow and the other plants shown grow beside the water. Their roots are implanted in the wet earth. The plants illustrated on these two pages have many species, all of which vary in height and habitat. But all the species have some outstanding characteristics in common. The sneezeweeds have yellow flower heads, often with dark discs. The bitterweed, a member of the sneezeweed group, grows in pastures. If cows eat it, it makes them give bitter-tasting milk. When the ripe seed pods of the jewelweeds are touched, they "explode."

SPATTERDOCK
WHITE WATER LILY
BUR REED
ROSE MALLOW
PICKERELWEED

The flowers of the bouncing Bet range in color from white to pink and have a spicy odor. Another common name for the plant is soapwort, because of the lather the leaves form when crushed in water. The American Indians called the plant "white man's trail," because its seeds caught on the soles of their moccasins.

The dayflower got its name from the fact that the flowers expand only in the morning. The blossoms of all the American wild dayflowers are blue, or blue and white. These plants, especially those that grow in shady places, reach a height of up to three feet.

How do seeds get transported from place to place?

Plants have always been brought by people from one place to another. When Europeans began settling in America, they brought seeds and young plants of many kinds to their new homes. Among these were useful plants such as apple trees and wheat, and many plants that were grown for their scent and beauty such as sweet mignonette, pink-flowered bouncing Bet and many kinds of roses. In addition to the plants purposely brought to America, many were brought by accident. In the sacks filled with seeds of wheat were occasional seeds of plants that grew as weeds in the European wheat fields. In the pots of soil in which young rose and apple plants were brought, there may have been a few seeds of the other plants that had been growing in the European gardens and orchards.

Many seeds of the foreign plants became scattered throughout large areas of America. People ate apples from their orchards and tossed away the cores, which were full of seeds, as they walked along the roads and paths. Wild apple trees soon grew in many places. Dandelion seeds were blown by the wind from the garden to the fields, where they began to grow wild. People walked through their gardens, past their flower beds, and perhaps a little mud containing seeds of bouncing Bet stuck to their shoes and was scraped off along the roadside. Perhaps a robin, while searching for worms in the gardens

Of the twenty kinds of chickweed, the common chickweed is the only one that is widespread in fields and moist places. The seed of this plant is a favorite food for many birds.

where bouncing Bet grew, got some mud and seeds on its feet or bill. Then the robin cleaned off the mud and seeds after it had flown to another place. Whichever way it happened, bouncing Bet "escaped" from the gardens and grew wild in the fields and along the roadsides.

Roses brought from Europe were not easy to grow from seeds, and they did not begin to grow outside of the gardens the way bouncing Bet did. The wild roses in America are a kind that had grown in the United States long before Europeans came.

What is an adventive?

Plants that are brought — accidentally or on purpose — to a place where they did not grow originally and where they become wild, are said to be *adventives*. Since they are usually plants that grow quickly and easily, and that scatter many seeds over a large area, they often become very annoying weeds. Among the many plants that people sometimes wish had never been brought to America are the dandelion, chickweed and devil's paintbrush, which are all from Europe, and the dayflower, which came from Asia.

Functions of the Different Parts of a Plant

Why do plants need roots?

In the soil in which plant roots grow are bits of minerals that have been chipped off rocks. In the soil there is also water that dissolves small amounts of these minerals. Have you ever dissolved salt in water? Soon after salt is put into a glass of water, it dissolves and cannot be seen. But it can be tasted! Other minerals do not dissolve so quickly, and if you put a pebble into water you would not see any difference in its size from day to day. Even so, it is dissolving, but *very* slowly.

Plant roots serve many purposes, but the most important thing they do is to soak up water and dissolved minerals from the soil. The plant needs the water and minerals to make its food. Once the food is made, the plant might store some of it in the root to be used later. The squirrel-corn plant always does this, and squirrels dig up these plants to eat the parts of the roots that have been thickened by stored food.

Roots are also needed for holding a plant firmly in the ground. Without strong roots spreading through the soil, there would be few plants on mountain tops and along the seashore, for the strong wind there would blow the plants away.

ROOT
ROOT HAIR
ROOTLETS

Plant with roots, rootlets and root hair.

FLOWERS OF THE DESERTS

Most of the flowering plants of the desert or desert-like areas belong to the CACTUS family, which has more than a thousand members. All of these plants are especially equipped to live in their surroundings. Unlike the leaves found in other plants, cactus plants have many sharp spines with little or no surface from which water could be lost by evaporation. Practically all have a fleshy stem that makes up the major part of the plant. These stems have vast water-storage spaces, which are filled whenever it rains. Many members of the cactus family are quite small, but some, such as the saguaro, reach up to seventy feet and often have as many as fifty branching arms. Most cacti grow in the warmer parts of the Americas, especially in Mexico and the dry regions of South America. Some species grow in Africa. Most cactus flowers are brightly colored and very large. They usually develop directly from the stems, and only rarely do they have flower stalks. Cacti are often cultivated in rock gardens and in houses.

The golden barrel cactus, a native of central Mexico, is symmetrical in shape and grows up to four feet high. The prickly poppy has fragile petals that range in color from white to lavender. Its leaves are very prickly. The queen of the night has a beautiful flower that blooms only at night. The Indian paintbrush splashes its bright red color everywhere. The jumping cactus does not jump, but *you* might, because loose stems leap up and sting painfully when stepped on. The roots of the yucca, a cactus that can be pollinated only by one species of moth, were used by the American Indians for soap.

DESERT MARIGOLD

GOLDEN BARREL CACTUS

MERRY WIDOW CACTUS

JUMPING CACTUS

GOLD POPPY

Of what use are stems?

Stems are like bundles of very thin pipes. They carry water and minerals from the roots to the leaves. They also carry food from the leaves to all other parts of the plant, so that the plant can continue to grow.

Many plants have stems with special functions. Morning-glories have long thin stems that twist around and climb up over other plants. This brings the leaves of the morning-glory out of the shade of nearby plants and into the sunlight. Wild strawberries have very short stems from which the leaves and flowers grow. But some of the branches of the short stems grow very long and creep over the ground for several feet. At the ends of the creeping stems grow more short, leafy stems. These develop roots that grow down into the soil, and they become new plants. The creeping stems allow the strawberry to spread and to become numerous without depending upon seeds.

The spring beauty stores extra food in a special, short fat stem that grows underground. Every spring this food is used to provide energy to send up green leaves and little sprays of pale pink flowers. The leaves make more food, and a large amount of it is sent back to the underground stem. During the summer, fall, and winter the leaves and flowers of the spring beauty wither away, and the underground stem rests until the next spring. Spring beauties grow in the woods, and the food stored in the stem gives them a head start. This allows them to grow quickly and blos-

The starchy, bulblike, underground stems of the spring beauty were used as food by the American Indians.

EPIDERMIS
CORTEX
STELE
PITH

Cross sections through a stem of a plant. They show the structure that enables a plant to carry liquids, which are collected by the roots, up to the leaves, where they are needed to manufacture the food for the plant. The epidermis is the protecting skin; the stele are the pipelines.

som early in the spring before the tree leaves are big enough to keep out the sunlight needed for making food.

Of what use are leaves?

Green leaves are very important because they make the essential food needed by plants and animals. The food that such leaves make is sugar. Sugar is made in all green parts of a plant, but, of course, leaves are mostly green parts. All that a green leaf needs to make sugar is sunlight, air and water. By adding the necessary dissolved minerals, which are obtained from the soil, plants can change sugar into other kinds of food.

Some animals eat green plants to get their food, as cows and zebras do when they eat grass and clover. Some animals eat other animals that have already eaten green plants, as lions do when they catch and eat a zebra. Whenever food is eaten, we can be sure that it derived from the sugar originally made in the green part of a plant.

What part does the flower play?

Certain parts of the flower become the fruit, which contains the seeds. Each fertile seed contains a baby plant, and food that it can use until it grows big enough to have its own roots and green leaves.

Flowers are made up of several different parts. There are the *sepals,* which are usually green. They are the parts that cover a flower bud. The *petals* are often large and brightly colored. They surround the *stamens,* which are threadlike and tipped with dustlike *pollen.* In the center there is usually a single *pistil.* It has a sticky tip that catches any pollen that lands there. Pollen is carried from one flower to another by the wind, or by insects, which are attracted by the petals and the scent. The insects are looking for sweet nectar, which is often formed at the base of the flower parts. But in order to drink the nectar, insects must brush against the stamens and pistil. When pollen from a certain kind of flower lands on the tip of a pistil of

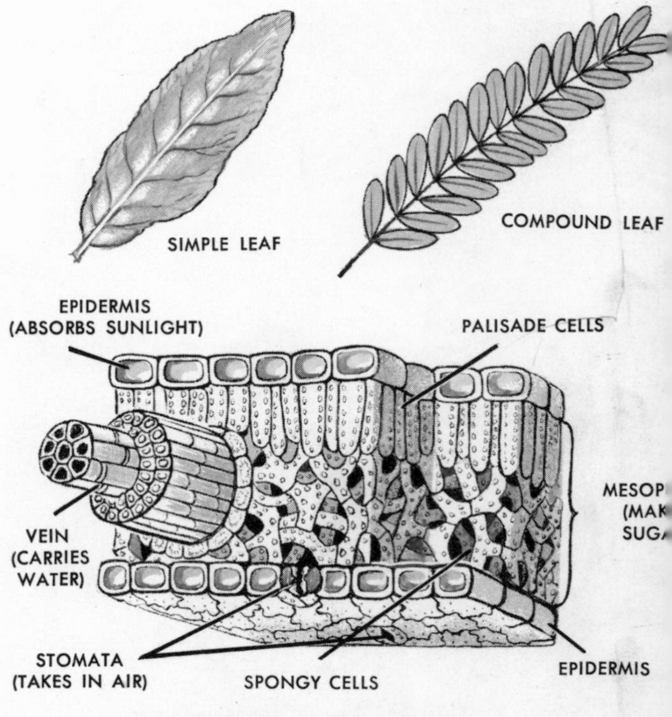

CROSS SECTION THROUGH LEAF

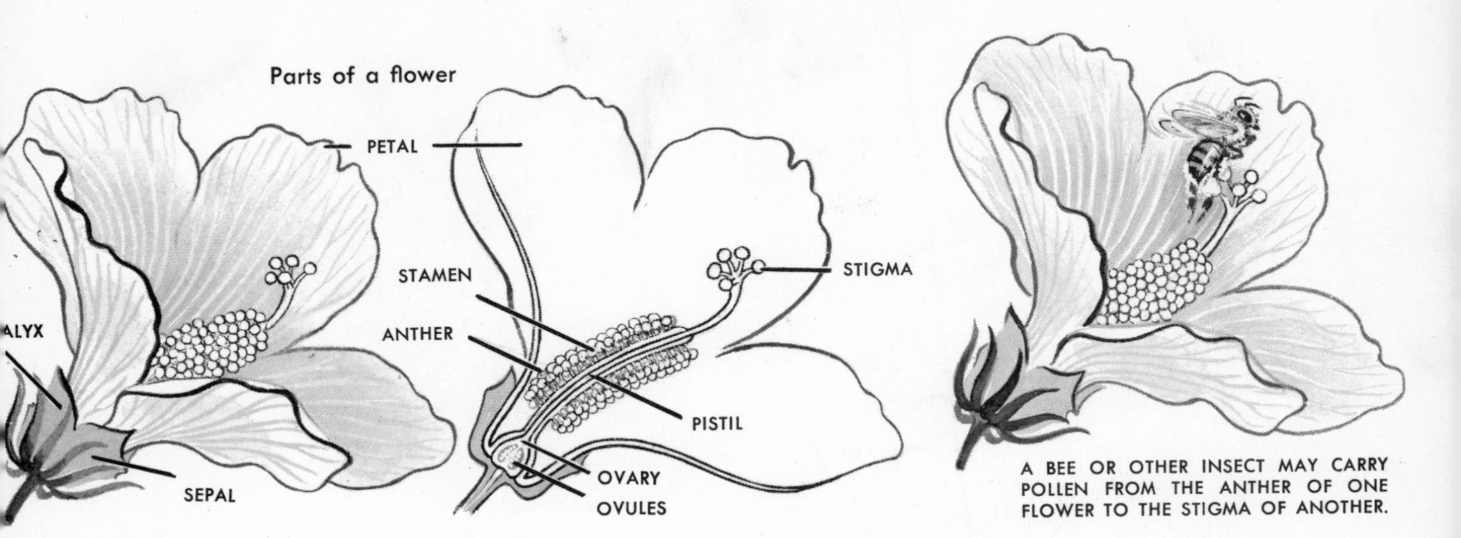

the same kind of flower, the pollen grows long tubes. These tubes reach down into the *ovary* at the bottom of the pistil. This makes the *seeds* form, and the outside of the ovary becomes the *fruit*.

The Value of Wild Flowers

Of what use are wild flowers to people?

Most of our countryside is beautiful for many reasons. We enjoy seeing the hills and lakes, the trees, grass and flowers, and the birds and animals, too.

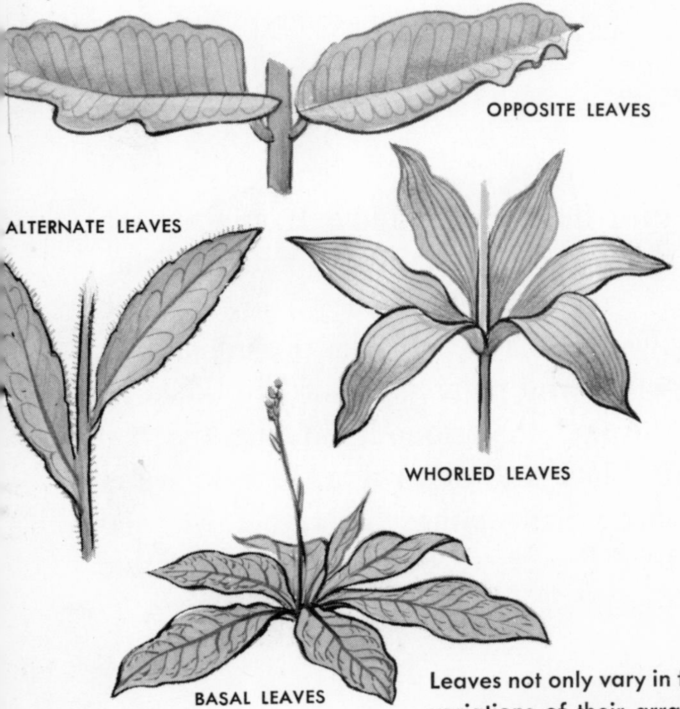

Leaves not only vary in form, but there are many variations of their arrangement on a stem.

A sunny field with thick green grass is beautiful at all times, but the field is more beautiful when it is sprinkled with white daisies and golden buttercups. Then, when autumn comes, the leaves of trees turn red, yellow and brown. Soon the old country roads are bordered by white and purple asters and yellow goldenrod. They are among the most beautiful sights to see.

There are many places, especially near our cities, where wild flowers no longer grow. They have been picked and uprooted and stepped upon until they are gone. Very often nothing is left beneath the trees except some soiled old papers and rusty tin cans that have been thrown there by careless persons. Nobody likes to see such places. We should all be careful never to turn a beautiful place into an ugly one.

How do flowers help to conserve valuable soil?

In addition to their beauty, wild flowers are very useful to us. If our hillsides were not covered with grasses, flowers, trees and bushes, the soil would be washed away whenever it rained. A road at the bottom of a hill would then be covered by the soil, or the soil would be carried into a lake or reservoir and turn the water muddy. It might wash down the mountainsides and cover up crops growing in a valley below, or even result in a flood. But this doesn't happen when wild plants spread their roots all through the ground, holding the soil in place and absorbing the rain water like a giant sponge. Therefore, we need wild flowers to help conserve valuable topsoil.

BARNYARD GRASS

The destruction of wild plant life, which provides food and shelter for many birds and other animals, can result in further damage to cultivated fields and gardens. You probably know that owls and foxes eat mice and rabbits. If there were no woods left, there wouldn't be any owls or foxes either. The farmer's fields would soon be overrun by mice, which eat the seeds; and by rabbits, which eat the leaves of plants. Of course, a fox sometimes catches an unprotected chicken, but without the fox there would be so many mice eating the chicken feed that there would be hardly enough left for the chickens themselves. This is only one of the very many cases where we need wild birds and animals and the wild plants that shelter and feed them.

How do plants affect animal and human life?

Many plants have strong fibers that we can use. When you eat a stalk of celery you probably notice the long threads that can be pulled off. Fibers similar to these can be used for making cloth and rope. Linen, for example, is woven from the fibers of flax stems. You may find flax, with its blue flowers, growing wild. We also use the fibers of Manila hemp, which comes from the tropical jungles of the Philippine Islands, and of agave, a desert plant from Mexico, to make rope and twine. Many years ago people made rope and cloth from the fibers of plants that grew wild in their own countries. Today we are able to grow fibrous plants from many parts of the world, as long as we have the proper climate. Flax is now grown in many nations, although it probably came originally from Asia.

What plant fibers can be used to make clothing and rope?

Wheat is a very important plant to us, because we make flour from its seeds and bread from the flour. It probably grew wild around the Eastern Mediterranean, but wheat has been cultivated for so long that it no longer looks like the original wild plant. When the first European people came to America, they brought wheat seeds with them to plant on their new farms. In some parts of America the European wheat grew very well. But when the pioneers began to farm in the colder northern areas, they found there was a good wheat crop only during certain years. That was when the winter frosts came late in the season. But there were many years when freezing weather killed the wheat before the seeds ripened.

How did Canadian scientists help to grow better wheat?

Canadian scientists found the answer by experimenting with wheat that ripened early. It was brought from northern Russia and the Himalayan Mountains in India. These varieties of wheat, needing only a short growing season, could be harvested before the early frosts. But they yielded small amounts of seeds that were not too good for making flour. By putting the pollen of one type of wheat on the pistils of another, seeds were obtained that combined the qualities of both types. The seeds were planted and the young plants were carefully watched. Plants of poor quality or with late-

WHEAT

TIMOTHY

BAMBOO

ripening seeds were thrown out. In 1903, after several years of this work, a plant was developed that combined the good qualities of both parents. The result was early-ripening seeds and heavy yields that were good for making flour. Soon this wheat was being grown in many parts of Canada and in the northern part of the United States. No longer do the farmers lose their wheat crop when the frosts are a little earlier than usual.

How are some plants useful to doctors?

In India and other parts of Asia grows a wild plant called rauwolfia. Its roots contain chemicals that are used in medicines to calm people who are very nervous and worried. It is also used by doctors to treat high blood pressure. Only a few years ago, scientists began to experiment with this plant, and they selected and grew plants whose roots produced more of the medicine than the average wild plant. These medicines can be fed to animals as well as to people. If they are put in the food of a wild animal, it will become more tame, for a while at least, and less nervous when people are nearby. In this way, a timid or ferocious animal that is sick can be calmed and treated by an animal doctor.

People have always obtained food, medicine and other products from different kinds of plants, and scientists are still discovering new uses for them.

PINK LADY-SLIPPER

Communities of Plants

Where do wild flowers grow?

Wild flowers grow just about everywhere on the land. Many even grow in marshes, lakes and rivers. We find them in hot, wet, tropical lands, in hot and dry deserts and at the edge of glacial ice. They grow high up on all but the very tallest mountain peaks, and they grow in sandy or pebbly soil along the seashore, although they do not grow in the sea itself. They grow in shady forests and in sunny fields. There are wild flowers in our gardens, although we usually call them weeds! They grow along the roadsides and even in the cracks of city pavements.

Of course, the wild flowers that grow next to glaciers are not the same kinds that grow in the desert. Flower seeds are scattered far and wide, but they grow only when they happen to come to the right place. If you were to collect seeds from water lilies and scatter them in the desert, it would be quite a waste of time, for they would not grow there.

PIPSISSEWA

ARBUTUS

FORGET-ME-NOT

SKUNK CABBAGE

ARROWHEAD

Some wild flowers have a very wide range. Dandelions, for example, grow practically all over the world. On the other hand, the Venus's-flytrap grows wild only in North and South Carolina.

Which wild flowers grow together?

Each kind of wild flower needs certain conditions to be able to grow. Those that have the same needs are likely to be found growing together. The flowers usually found in the woods are types that do most of their growing and blooming early in the spring before the tree leaves shade the ground. The top layer of soil is composed mostly of dead leaves that have fallen from the trees. Different kinds of leaves produce different types of soil, so the flowers in an oak wood are not always the same as those growing beneath maple trees. Oak, pine and hemlock woods often shelter pink lady-slipper, partridgeberry, trailing arbutus, mountain laurel and pipsissewa.

If there is a brook running through a meadow, the wet soil near its banks may be the home of the forget-me-not, cardinal flower, skunk cabbage and marsh marigold.

A shallow lake is a good spot for water lilies and spatterdock, spikes of arrowhead and pickerelweed, wild calla and golden club. If there is a bog at the edge of the lake, that is the place to look for sundews, pitcher plants and cranberries, as well as several kinds of orchids. No florist has flowers more beautiful than the grasspink, goldcrest, calypso or arethusa. These are just a few of the native orchids growing in bogs.

But as our cities grow bigger, our woods are destroyed, and wet lands are filled in to make room for more streets and buildings. In many places where wild orchids once grew, now only plantain, ragweed and crab grass grow in the cracks of concrete sidewalks.

How do winds and water currents help plant growth?

Plants produce seeds in large quantities. They are scattered about in various ways, and those that land in a suitable place begin to grow. Some seeds are carried far away by the wind. They have parts that are shaped like little sails or parachutes. If you blow upon dandelion or milkweed seeds, you will see how they float in the air.

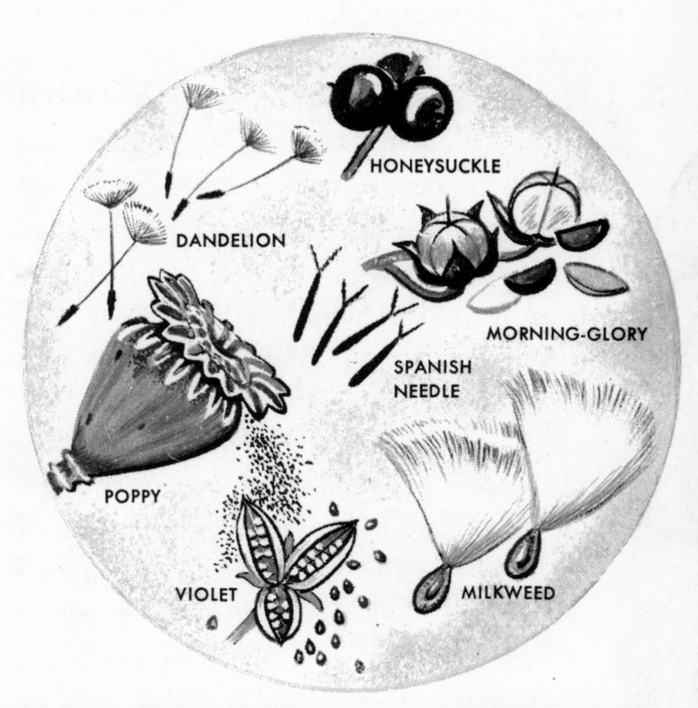

Seeds and seed containers come in many shapes and sizes.

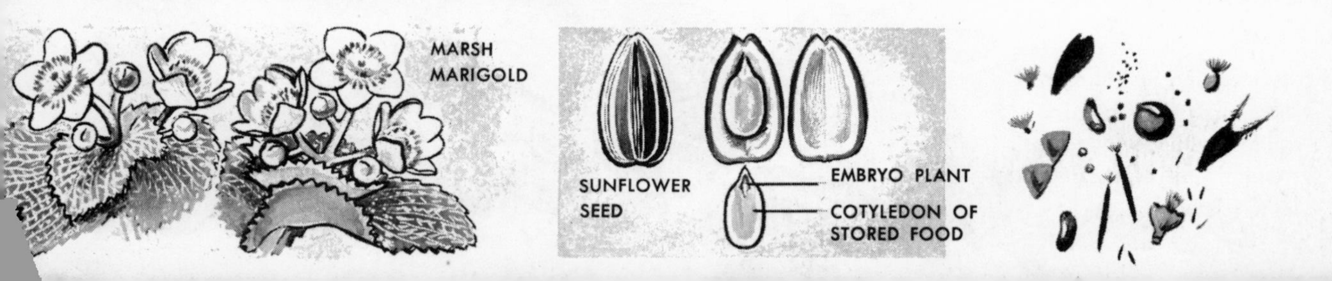

There are seeds that fall into the water and are carried from one place to another by waves and currents. Coconut seeds float easily and are often found growing wild along the seashore in warm tropical places.

How do birds scatter seeds?

Birds are responsible for scattering many types of seeds. If you have a cherry tree in your garden, you know how fond birds are of cherries. They swallow the seeds with the fruit, and since cherry seeds have a hard coat, they are not at all harmed by being in the bird's stomachs. After the soft fruit is digested, the bird may drop the seed a long way from the tree that produced it. Birds eat poison ivy berries and dogwood berries, and the seeds inside are scattered in the same way.

Mistletoe is a plant that grows on tree branches. It gets its food by sending suckers into the tree, since it cannot make its own food. A bird that has eaten mistletoe berries finds later that some of the sticky seeds have remained on its bill. It wipes its bill clean on the tree branch to which it has flown, and this is enough to "plant" the seeds in a new place.

In what ways do animals help to produce plants?

Have you ever watched a gray squirrel burying acorns or other nuts? Acorns are the seeds of oak trees, and in the winter the squirrel digs up those that it buried in the autumn. In this way the squirrel has enough food at a time when it would otherwise be scarce, but the animal has also provided for new oaks by overlooking some of the acorns which had been hidden. These acorns are comfortably planted in loose soil or under a thick layer of dead leaves.

Some seeds are "hitchhikers." They have hooks that catch onto a passing animal's fur or a person's clothing. When the animal notices them, it scratches and bites until the seeds drop to the ground where they may grow. When a dog has burrs sticking to its hair, its owner combs or pulls them out. If the burrs are dropped in the garden, there will be extra weeding to do. You may have found burrs sticking to your socks after walking by these plants.

What flowers plant their own seeds?

There are some types of flowers whose fruits throw out their ripe seeds for some distance — without depending upon wind, animals or anything else. The touch-me-not, which grows along roadsides and in thin woods, has fruits that split into little slingshots when touched, flinging the seeds about in all directions. Ripe violet fruits split into three sections, each containing many seeds. The sec-

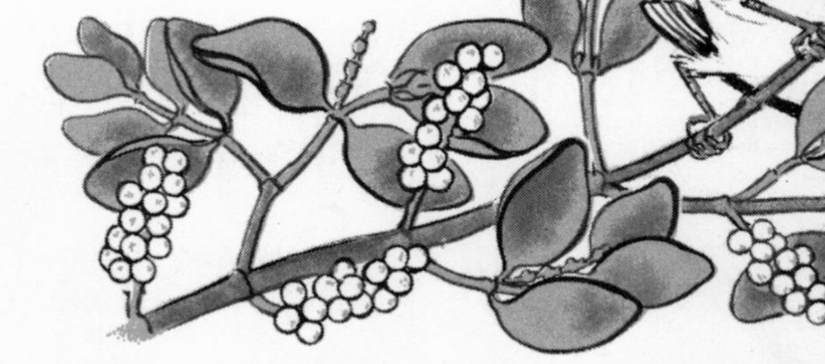

By cleaning its bill on a tree branch, a bird quite involuntarily may "plant" the seeds of a new mistletoe plant.

While the seeds of some flowers, such as clematis and fireweed, drift like gliders in the wind, the seeds of the tumbleweed are scattered as they roll along the ground.

tions dry out and begin to curl up, pressing against the seeds until they are popped out like marbles pressed between two fingers. If you find violet fruits that are still closed and put them into a paper bag, they will ripen and split within a day or two. You can even hear the seeds shooting out against the paper. But don't leave violet fruits uncovered in the house or you will find the seeds all over the floor for a distance of several feet. Squirting cucumber is another fruit that propels its seeds. The fruits, which are full of juice and seeds,

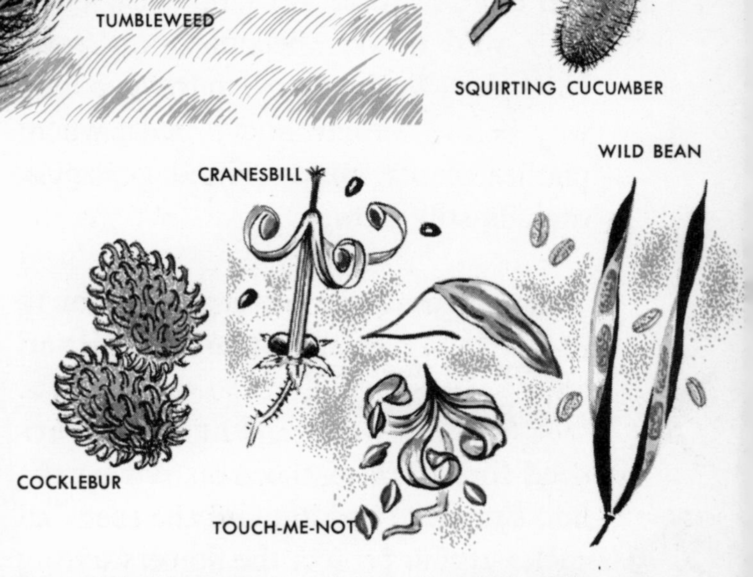

The squirting cucumber, cocklebur, cranesbill, touch-me-not, wild bean and many other plants "explode" their seeds when they are ripe.

open at one end when they are ripe. The outside of the fruit presses upon the inside, and the seeds come squirting out.

Protecting Our Wild Flowers

Why are many wild flowers becoming rare?

There used to be a time when people could build and farm only upon suitable land. Swamps, rocky hillsides and sandy regions were left alone, and so were the wild flowers that grew there. But now we are able to change such land. With modern machinery we can drain water away from a swamp, or we can fill it with extra rocks and soil until it becomes dry land. Bulldozers can push rocks and trees away, leaving the land flat and clear.

You can see that when a swamp is dried out and it becomes a place with houses and shops and gardens, the wild flowers that used to live there are gone. Almost all of the flowers are covered by the extra soil and buildings, but even those that are left untouched, die when the soil becomes dry. Wild flowers that live in a swamp need wet soil. As more and more of these wet lands disappear, their wild flowers become more rare. Nowadays we may have to travel a long way before we can find a place where pitcher plants, sundews and grasspink orchids still grow.

How do trees help to protect flowers?

When the trees of a forest are cut down, the woodland flowers die. These flowers need the shade of the trees during the hot summer, and the leaves that fall each autumn protect the flowers during the winter. On the dead and crumbling leaves and wood grow clumps of ghostly white Indian pipes. Where the soil of the forest floor is partly composed of rotting oak leaves, colonies of dainty pink lady-slipper orchids may be found. When the trees are gone, so are the woodland flowers.

What are the conditions under which certain flowers grow?

In their place are different flowers that grow well under the new conditions. If houses and lawns take the place of the woods, dandelions, chickweed and white clover will become common. These pretty wild flowers grow in sunny places and stay close to the ground, so a lawn mower does not harm them. They do so well in the lawn, in fact, that they crowd out the grass. If the trees are cut and the land is not used for building purposes, field flowers such as the daisy, black-eyed Susan and goldenrod will begin to appear. These species can grow among tall grasses, for they are big enough to get their share of the sunlight.

The wild flowers that are rare, or in great danger of becoming so, are those that grow in the marshes and woodlands. These are the wild flowers whose homes are being destroyed. Field flowers and those that can grow in lawns and gardens are, in many cases, becoming more common than they used to be, because we are actually providing more homes for them. Every time we drain swamps or cut down trees and build houses, we are also building homes for dandelions. Every time we cut down trees to create a field, we are building good homes for daisies.

Does it harm a plant to pick its flowers?

Whether or not it is harmful to a plant to pick its flowers depends upon the plant. In all cases, picking flowers prevents the seeds from forming, and that means there will be fewer seeds to grow into new plants. This does not matter if the plant is common. But in many states, there are some plants so rare that laws have been passed forbidding anyone to pick them. Hepatica and trailing arbutus are among the plants protected in the State of New York. You can find out which flowers should not be picked in your state, even if there is no specific law forbidding it, by writing a letter to Wild Flower Preservation Society, Inc., Washington 15, D. C. Sometimes it takes a long time to pass such laws, and in the meantime certain flowers may be almost completely wiped out. Before you pick wild flowers, therefore, be sure that you know their names and whether or not the Wild Flower Preservation Society has asked us to leave them alone. There are field-guide books, with pictures of wild flowers, that include common and scientific names. Several of these books are probably available at your school or local library.

Some flowers have very short stems, and when people pick them they usually take part of the rest of the plant, too. Dogwood trees have beautiful leaves, but the only way to pick them is to cut off a whole branch that has taken years to grow. If too many people did this, we would soon lose the sight of lovely drifts of white dogwood leaves in the spring. In Pennsylvania, it is against the law to pick wild dogwood for this very reason. Trillium is another plant with short-stemmed flowers, and in this case each plant has one flower with three large leaves just below it. Picking a trillium flower means picking all the leaves of the plant. This does double damage, for there will be no seeds to form new plants. In addition, the loss of the leaves means that no more food can be made, and the whole plant soon dies. No plant can survive if all or most of its leaves are picked, but if it has many leaves it will not hurt if a few are taken. Long, leafy stems of bright fireweed and fragrant meadowsweet, with spikes of flowers at their tips, can be cut without harming the plants.

PEAR BLOSSOM

Recognizing Wild Flowers

What are "plant families"?

Closely related plants are grouped into families, just as animals are. You can tell that a lion is more like a cat than a dog. In the same way, you can see that an apple tree is more like a pear tree than a pine, and that a daisy is more like a black-eyed Susan than a wild rose. But did you know that apples and strawberries are both in the rose family? The plants look quite different at first, but if you look at the blossoms, you will see that they

STRAWBERRY

APPLE BLOSSOM

are very much alike. Each flower usually has five sepals and five petals, arranged in the same way, with many yellow stamens in the center. Some garden roses have many petals, but the wild ones generally have five. The scientists who study plants have been able to tell us which plants belong to which family.

What are composites?

The composite family contains plants such as daisies, asters and sunflowers. The flower head of each composite is made up of many tiny flowers packed closely together. Usually the inner flowers, called *disk flowers,* have very small petals. The outer flowers in the head are called *ray flowers.* Lettuce is one of the few edible composite plants.

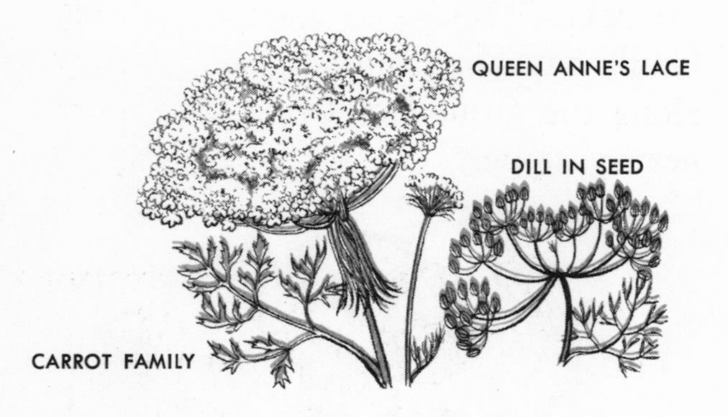

How can flowers of the carrot family be recognized?

The carrot family is an interesting one, especially to people who like to cook. Many of its members have seeds that are very spicy, such as caraway, anise and dill. The wild Queen Anne's lace, from which carrots were developed, belongs in this family. You can recognize members of the group by the arrangement of their flowers. The flower stem is divided at the top into several branches, each of which may also be divided into branches with the flowers at their tips. This gives a lacy, umbrella-like look to the flower cluster.

What are the differences between the buttercup and rose families?

The buttercup family is similar to the rose family in that its petals and sepals are usually present in groups of five each, and the center of the flower is filled with many yellow stamens. But there are differences, too. Members of the buttercup family may have no petals at all, and the sepals are often brightly colored and look like petals instead of being green. Also, while the petals and sepals of buttercups are attached to the flower stem *below* the bottom of the pistils, the rose family has its petals attached halfway up around the middle of the pistil's ovary. Perhaps these differences seem small, but to the scientist who is trying to determine which plants are related to each other, they are as important as the difference between fur and feathers.

But the similarities between members of the rose and buttercup families tell us that these two groups are more closely related to each other than they are to orchids or composites. In the same way, we see that cats are more closely related

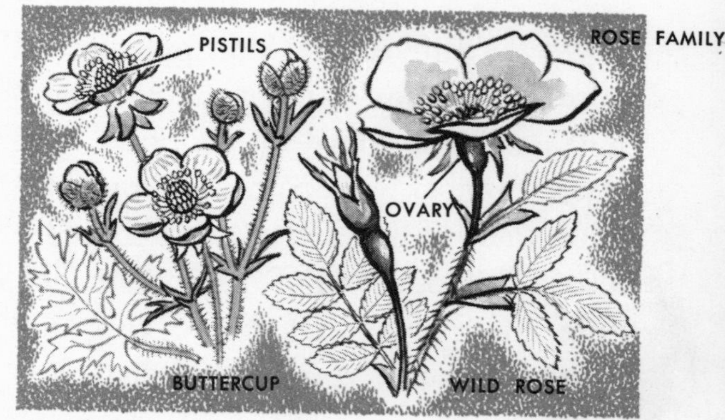

to lions, and dogs are more closely related to wolves than they are to horses or mice. All plants and animals have distant relatives as well as close ones.

ORCHID FAMILY

YELLOW LADY-SLIPPER

Why are insects so important to flowers of the orchid family?

The orchid family has many more members than any other plant family. Some grow in forests and swamps, but most live in tropical jungles. Several American-grown orchids have big beautiful flowers, such as the grasspink, goldcrest orchid, showy orchid and yellow lady-slipper. Others, such as lady's-tresses and the leafy green orchid, have spikes of rather inconspicuous flowers. But even the smallest are interesting to look at because of their unusual shape. Orchid flowers have three sepals and three petals. Unlike most flowers, the petals are sometimes green and the sepals are sometimes of another color. One petal is larger than the others and is often beautifully colored and strangely shaped. It is called the *lip*. In the lady-slipper orchids, this larger petal forms a pouch in which there is a little sweet nectar. Bees and other insects that force their way into the pouch in order to drink the nectar brush past the yellow pollen. The pollen sticks to their bodies and is brushed off on the next orchid flower that an insect visits. Without pollen-carrying insects, orchid flowers would not form seeds.

What kind of stems do flowers of the morning-glory family have?

The flowers of the morning-glory family have all their petals attached to each other, forming a funnel. Each petal has a rib along its center, and if you count the ribs you will see that there are five petals. Most of the members of this family have long thin stems that creep along the ground or twine about any nearby support.

MORNING-GLORY FAMILY

MORNING-GLORY

How can you identify members of the pea family?

Most members of the pea family also have flowers with five petals, but the petals are not all the same size or shape. The fruits are sometimes very big and sometimes

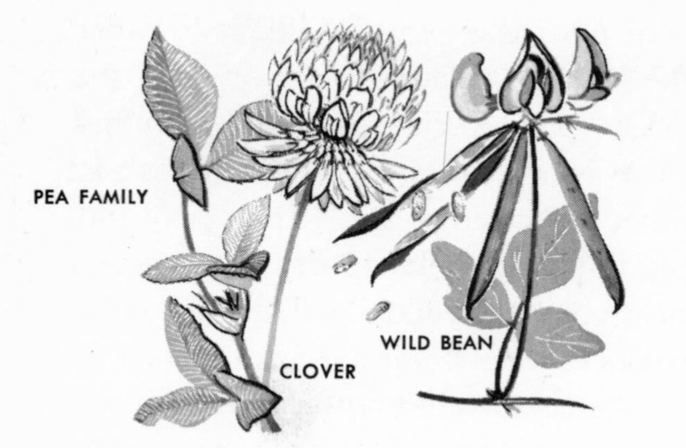

quite small, but they are always shaped like the familiar pea pod or string bean. If you examine a clover blossom, you will notice that it is made of many tiny flowers set closely together. Each flower is shaped like a sweet pea. Those at the bottom are the first to flower and the first to form the tiny fruits or pods.

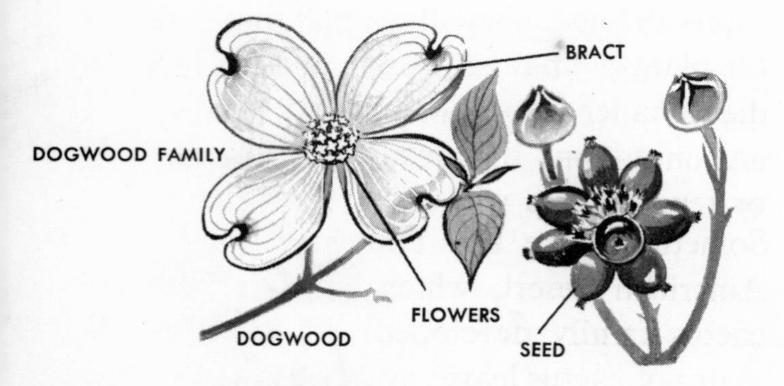

How many members does the dogwood family have?

Both the dogwood tree and the tiny creeping bunchberry belong to the dogwood family. These two plants have clusters of small greenish yellow flowers surrounded by four large white *bracts*. Bracts are a special kind of leaf, but people usually think they are petals. These fall off after a while just as petals do, and the flower pistils form a group of red berries, which are the fruit. In spite of the difference in size between dogwood and bunchberry, they are easily seen to be closely related. The dogwood family has only ninety members. (There are more than 15,000 members of the orchid family and 3,200 members of the rose family.)

What do changes do for a plant?

There are constant slight changes appearing in all plants. This does not mean that a single plant with wide leaves suddenly grows narrower leaves, although that happens occasionally. Of the many seeds produced by a plant, most grow into seedlings with leaves identical to those of the parent plant; some will have slightly narrower leaves and some will have slightly wider ones. Most of the changes that occur are not very important. But sometimes the changes make it impossible for the plant to continue to live, and sometimes they help it to live longer or grow better than others of its kind.

How does color affect plant life?

Sometimes there is a change in the color of the flowers. Suppose there is a plant with red flowers that open only at night. Of the many seeds produced, one might grow up into a white-flowered plant. Now, there are some insects that fly about at night, visiting flowers in the hope of finding nectar, and at the same time, carrying pollen from one flower to another. These insects can see white flowers more easily than red ones, so the white-flowered plant will be likely to produce more seeds than its red-flowered relatives. Of the plants that will grow from these seeds, quite a few may also be white-flowered. As years go by, the white-flowered plants may outnumber those with red flowers.

But what would happen if this change in flower color took place in a plant whose flowers opened only during the day? Red flowers are seen as easily as white ones by many insects that fly by day. The plant with white flowers would then have no advantage.

Can you imagine what would happen if a seed grew into a plant with white *leaves?* Of course, there are many plants with leaves that are *partly* white, such as green and white ivy, or plants with a few special white leaves, such as the dogwood. But a plant must have some green parts in order to make its food. Every now and then a seed sprouts into a new plant that has no green color at all. The seedling lives for a while on the food stored in the seed, but when that is used up, it dies.

What are mutations?

These changes that suddenly appear in plants are called *mutations.* They occur in great numbers, year after year, and are passed on to new generations. After many, many years, perhaps thousands of years, there may have been enough mutations in one group of plants to make it quite different from what it was before. Sometimes a group of plants grows throughout the whole of a certain area, and something happens to separate them. Perhaps a glacier came down from the north, killing all the plants beneath it, while the plants continued to grow on both sides of the glacier. There is little chance that the mutations will be exactly the same in both groups. If the glacier remains for a long enough time, the two groups, once of the same kind, will become more and more different. Groups of plants that developed in different ways a long, long time ago are called *families.*

Perhaps in a certain region, as centuries pass, there is less and less rain, and the land slowly becomes drier. Since leaves lose a lot of moisture from their surfaces, using only a part of what they receive from the roots to make sugar, the plants with many large leaves would die. Smaller leaves lose less water, and any mutations that result in narrower or fewer leaves will be of great value. Something like this happened in the American desert, which is where the cactus family developed. All that remains of cactus leaves are sharp thorns.

DESERT LANDSCAPE WITH CACTI

HEDGEHOG CACTUS

OPUNTIA

Some Strange and Unusual Wild Flowers

Are there plants that eat insects?

We are used to the fact that many insects eat plants, but we are surprised when we first find out that some plants "eat" insects! Of course, these plants have no mouths or stomachs and do not really eat anything. But they trap small insects in their leaves and use them for food. These plants have green leaves and make sugar for food. They can live and grow without ever catching insects. But perhaps they grow a bit better when they have an occasional meal of meat. We are not quite sure of this yet. They all happen to grow in very wet soil where few other plants can exist. Some scientists think that their ability to use insects as food may help them to survive in the mud of the marshes where they live.

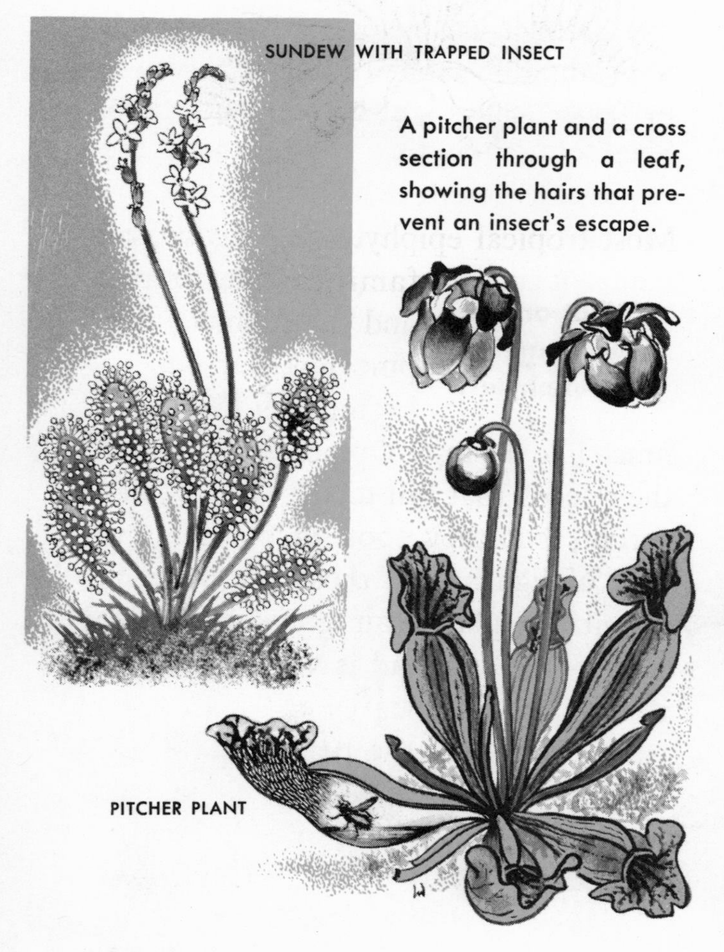

A pitcher plant and a cross section through a leaf, showing the hairs that prevent an insect's escape.

What is the largest insect-eating plant?

The pitcher plant is the largest of these carnivorous, or meat-eating, plants. The common kind has dark maroon flowers in June. Its leaves are shaped, as you can guess from the name, like pitchers. In the bottom of each pitcher is rain water and digestive chemicals that the plant produces. It is something like the digestive juices in our own stomachs. These chemicals dissolve the insects so that they can be absorbed by the plant. Stiff hairs, all pointing down, line the top part of the inside of the leaf-pitchers. Any insect that crawls in finds itself sliding downhill on the hairs. If it tries to walk up, the sharp tips of these hairs are all pointing at it. It is definitely a one-way trip, and at the end the insect drowns in the water and is digested.

Sundews are very small plants that are quite common in bogs and swamps. Each leaf is covered with sticky hairs. A small insect that touches the hairs is caught fast, and the whole leaf soon closes around it and digests it. Sundews have small white flowers in the summer.

Can an insect escape the Venus's-flytrap?

The Venus's-flytrap grows wild only in marshes in North and South Carolina, but it is often sold by plant nurseries that grow it from seed. It has little

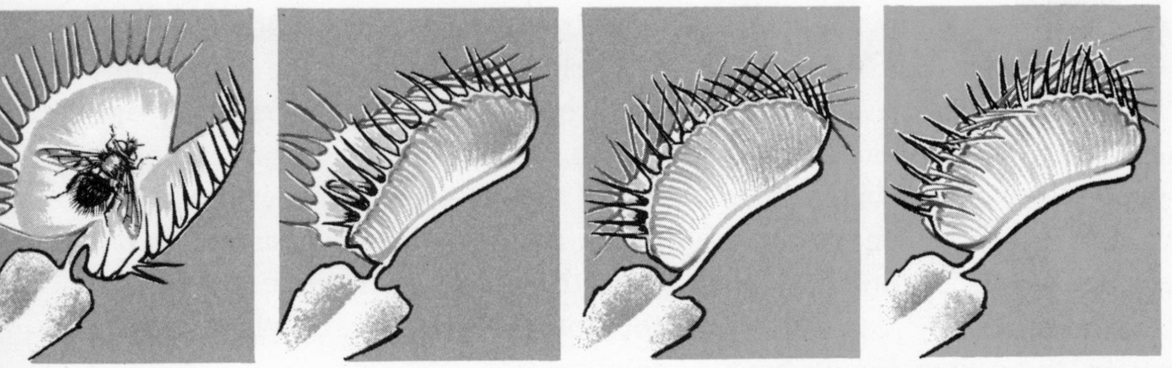

Here are four phases of a Venus's-flytrap catching an insect. The closing of the leaves is a very rapid action.

white flowers in May. Its fringed leaves are hinged down the center. Each half-leaf has three hairs near the hinge, and if they are touched the leaf closes. Insects that walk along the leaf and touch the hairs are trapped. Strong insects, like bumblebees, just push their way out, but weaker ones are caught and digested. If you ever see a plant of Venus's-flytrap, you can watch the trap work by touching the hairs with your finger.

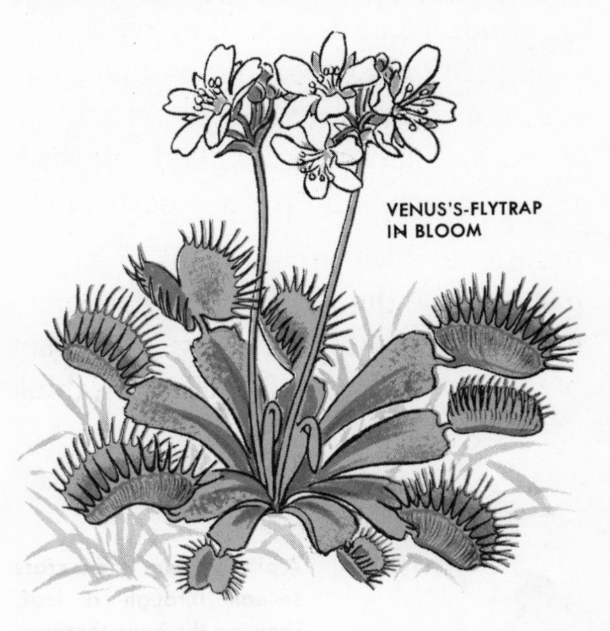

VENUS'S-FLYTRAP IN BLOOM

Are there plants that do not grow in the ground?

Not all plants are rooted in the ground. Some grow perched on tree branches high in the air and are called *epiphytic* plants. Epiphytic plants are found in tropical climates, in places such as jungles. Only here is the air so humid — so full of water vapor — that these plants can get enough water without being rooted in the damp soil. Since so many tropical plants are tall and large-leaved, and they grow so close together in a hot wet climate, the plants growing close to the ground get very little sunlight. But the epiphytes sitting high in the topmost tree branches get all the sunlight they need. They do no harm to the trees.

What are the two families of epiphytes?

Most tropical epiphytes belong to two families, the orchid and the bromeliad or pineapple family. The bromeliads look very much like the tops of pineapples. Any of their seeds that fall to the ground may sprout, but they soon die because of lack of light. Only those that land in a suitable place can grow well. The stem of a bromeliad is very short, and its tuft of long leaves often forms a cuplike shape at the bottom. This cup catches and holds quite a bit of rain water.

Spanish moss, which, in the southern

part of the United States, hangs in long gray masses from trees and telephone wires, is a member of the bromeliad family. The pineapple plant itself, which has a thick juicy stem on which the flowers grow, is one of the bromeliads that grows with its roots in the ground. The pineapple flowers do not develop into fruits and seeds.

Members of the orchid family have very tiny seeds that are blown about by the wind, which is how they reach the treetops. Orchid roots grow along the tree branch and between the cracks in the bark. This keeps the plant attached to the branch. The roots absorb moisture from the air and from the damp tree bark.

The orchids that grow on the ground are called TERRESTRIAL ORCHIDS, while those that grow perched on trees are called EPIPHYTIC ORCHIDS.

Many orchids have greenish roots that can make sugar. There is even one group of orchids that has no leaves or stems, but only roots and flowers. Its green roots make all its food.

Orchids grow all over the world. Only the tropical species are generally epiphytic. Those that grow in other climates are rooted in the ground. Not every orchid flower is beautiful, but even the tiniest of them is shaped like the florist's orchids with which we are familiar.

What kind of flowers live in the water?

Many wild flowers live in the water. They are called *aquatic* plants. Some of these, such as the beautiful white water lily and the yellow spatterdock, grow with their roots in the mud of a lake bottom. Their long-stemmed leaves and flowers float upon the surface of the water. The blue-flowered pickerelweed and the bright yellow golden club also grow in shallow water with their roots in the mud below.

The water hyacinth grows in southern streams and rivers. Its hollow air-filled leaf-stems float on the surface of the water, holding up the green leaves and pale purple flowers. The roots do not need sand or mud, and so the water hyacinth can grow in rivers that are too deep for water lilies and other aquatic plants. In some places, it spreads across the entire water surface so thickly that boats cannot sail through it.

The bladderworts live in shallow water. Their branching green stems float beneath the surface, sending up stalks with yellow or purple flowers in the summer. The leaves and roots of these stems are very tiny, and in some kinds of bladderwort they may be missing altogether. Upon the submerged stems

SPANISH MOSS

BROMELIAD

WATER HYACINTHS

VICTORIA REGIA

The Victoria Regia is a water lily whose leaves grow as large as seven feet in diameter. One leaf could easily carry the weight of a man.

grow little hollow bladders that trap and digest tiny water insects and other small animals. These bladders provide the plant with part of its food as well as with its name.

What plants live upon dead plants?

Plants that are not green cannot make their own food. They have to get food from other plants — either live ones or dead ones. Plants that grow upon dead plants are called *saprophytes*. Mushrooms are saprophytes. Perhaps you have seen them growing upon fallen logs and branches. Some grow in the soil, using the dead plant matter in it for food.

There are a few flowering plants that are saprophytes. Indian pipes grow on dead wood and leaves in forests. They form graceful clumps of short stems, each covered with tiny scale-like leaves and ending in a nodding bell-shaped flower. The whole plant — leaves, stems and flowers — is pure white, but it turns black in spots if it is picked or even touched, so it should be left alone. The red pinesaps are close relatives of the Indian pipes and grow in the same manner.

INDIAN PIPE

A few of the orchids, called coral-roots, are leafless saprophytes. Their small orange or purplish flowers are found in forests or at the edge of swamps. These orchids have branching underground stems that look like coral, and they send up flowering stalks in the spring and summer.

What plants live upon living plants?

Plants that grow upon living plants are called *parasites*. Quite a few of the flowering plants are parasites that are nourished by absorbing food from the juice of another living plant. They seldom do much harm to the plant on which they grow. The ghost pipe is a tiny grayish plant with little lavender flowers. It gets its food from the roots of other plants. A similar plant, the squawroot, has yellow flowers and absorbs food from the roots of oak trees. A taller relative of these plants is the beechdrops, and it lives upon the roots of beech trees. Ghost pipes, squawroot and beechdrops are all members of the broomrape family. There are other members, too, and all of them are parasites with no green coloring at all.

Dodder is a parasitic relative of the morning-glory that twines its bright yellow or orange stems around other plants. A dodder seedling begins to grow normally, but when it touches another plant its stem sends little rootlike projections into it; the dodder root withers away. These projections absorb the food that the parasite cannot make for itself. The dodder has clusters of tiny white flowers. Some kinds live only upon one particular plant, such as the flax dodder. As its name tells us, it lives only upon flax plants.

How can plants live in a desert?

The hot dry climate of a desert makes plant life very difficult, but those plants that have become adapted to desert life can no longer live under other conditions. Desert plants have long root systems that quickly soak up water whenever it becomes available, which isn't often. They are unlike other plants whose thin leaves and stems lose most of the moisture sent up from the roots. In desert plants, all water that is not needed immediately to make food is stored inside the thick juicy leaves or stems, to be used during the driest part of the year. If a tropical plant were to be transplanted to a desert, its leaves would lose more moisture than its roots could find and absorb, and the whole plant would soon dry up and die. Desert plants do most of their growing and blossoming after a rain. At other times they grow very slowly, if at all, as trees do in winter.

Are all desert plants in the cactus family?

Plants belonging to many families, including those in the cactus family, have become adapted to desert life. Some, such as haworthia and gasteria, belong to the lily family and grow wild in African deserts. The carpetweed family has a few desert members that look more like grayish green rocks and pebbles than like plants. These "stone plants" grow in South Africa, sometimes half-buried by sand. When they bloom, the flowers grow on short stems that push

Growing in the shadow of a beech tree one may find cancer root (also called ghost pipe), and broomrape.

BROOMRAPE

CANCER ROOT

The large coral root is an orchid of the coral root family. It can be found growing at the edge of a swamp and in the forest.

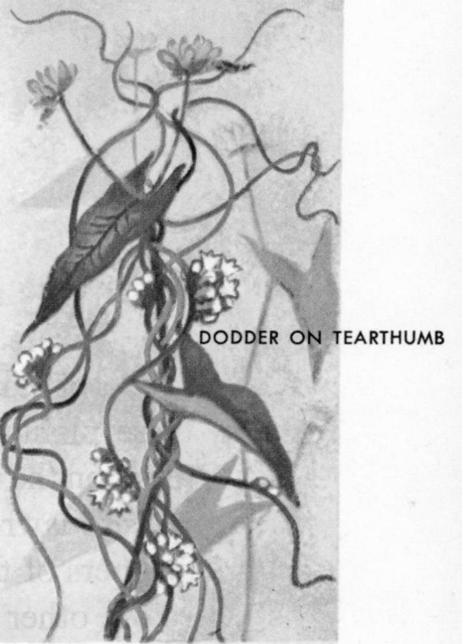

The tiny, bell-shaped blossoms of the dodder belong to a plant that has neither leaves nor roots.

GASTERIA

STONE PLANT (CARPETWEED FAMILY)

HAWORTHIA

Not all flowers that live in the desert belong to the cactus family. Many plants that live in the dry parts of Africa have developed thick leaves in which water is stored just as the cacti store water in their thick stems. Some African plants, brought to America in "dish gardens," are able to grow successfully.

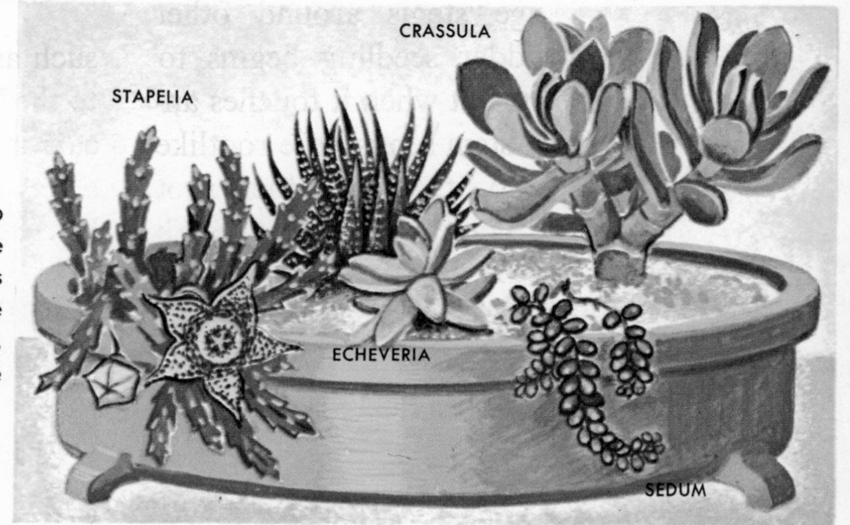

up from between two hard, thick, juicy leaves. Without looking closely, one would think that the flowers were growing from a crack in a rock!

The cactus family originally grew only in America, but some of its members now grow wild in other parts of the world to which people have brought them. The thorns of a cactus are all that remain of the leaves, and it is the thick green stem that stores moisture and manufactures food.

The cactus plants developed their present form through many, many years of mutations. Each time that a new plant happened to be able to live with less water than other plants needed, it was perhaps able to live longer than others in the dry climate. It had time to form more seeds, too, and some of them were scattered into still drier places where only the smallest-leaved seedlings could survive. The members of the cactus family that kept the original leaf type have all died out, except for pereskia, which lived in wetter areas.

"Taming" the Wild Flowers

What do wild flowers need in order to grow?

If you have a garden, you might want to try growing wild flowers. Some of them are very difficult to grow, but some grow well in gardens — and

BLACK-EYED SUSAN

EVENING PRIMROSE

others grow too well! Those are the ones that become weeds. They grow so easily and spread so quickly that we have to spend a lot of time pulling out the extra plants.

All wild flowers have certain needs. They must have the proper climate, the right amount of rain and sunshine, and

the correct type of soil. You may be sure that any flowers growing wild in your neighborhood will have the right climate in your garden. If you were to take a trip hundreds of miles to the south, you would see wild flowers that would find your garden too cold in the winter; and if you were to travel north, you would see some plants that would find your garden too hot in the summer.

Which wild flowers do well in gardens?

If you have a sunny garden you can grow wild flowers from the nearby fields and roadsides. Among the easiest are vervain, black-eyed Susan, goldenrod, butterfly weed (or orange milkweed), blue-eyed grass, pasqueflower, spring larkspur, wild strawberry, evening primrose, midland shooting star and bluet.

If your garden is very shady, ferns and woodland flowers might do well there. Some of the best kinds to grow are merrybell, bloodroot, Solomon's-seal, Solomon's-plume, alumroot, wild columbine, hepatica, violets of many kinds, jewel shooting star, spring beauty, rue anemone, jack-in-the-pulpit, Virginia bluebell and wild bergamot. Many of these may not be picked when they are found wild, but the plants and seeds can be bought from a flower nursery. Make sure that you do not dig up any plant that the Wild Flower Preservation Society tells us to leave alone.

How does soil affect plants?

The soil in which flowers grow is very important. There are many different types of soil. Some plants will grow in almost any kind of soil, but others have very particular requirements. Some soil is very sandy, some is made mostly of clay, some is composed mainly of dead rotted leaves (called leafmold), and some soil is a mixture of all these things. The leafmold in the soil can be formed from oak leaves, maple leaves, pine needles or any other kind of leaf. The sand and clay come from certain minerals that make up the rocks.

BLOODROOT

These are just a few of the many wild flowers you can "tame" for your garden. Try it; it can be fun.

Many wild flowers are difficult to grow because they need a very particular type of soil. If you have the proper spot for them, they should do well. You can see some of their requirements — whether they grow naturally only in sand or in wet soil. But you cannot know everything they need unless you make chemical tests on the soil. Many large nurseries sell "soil-testing kits" that have all the required equipment and directions for using it. In this way, you can test the soil in which any plant is growing when you find it wild or buy it. Then test your garden soil to see if it is suitable. If it isn't, the directions in the soil-testing kit tell you what to add to your soil. If you send a sample of the soil to your State Agricultural Experimental Station, they will test the soil for you.

FLOWERS OF THE WOODS

Most woodland flowers are unable to grow in strong sunlight, and all the flowers pictured on these two pages grow in the shaded areas of the woods. They flourish in a composition of soil that has been enriched by humus. Humus is a black or brown material that is formed by decaying matter. This matter includes leaves that have fallen to the earth, the rotting wood of trees and branches, the waste materials of forest animals, and the decomposing bodies of dead animals. Spring flowers bloom in the woodland before the sun becomes too bright. They make use of the sunshine that comes down to them through trees that are not yet fully leafed. Other woodland flowers, which bloom later, get enough sunshine from the rays that filter down through the foliage. It may be said, therefore, that the character of the tree in the forest influences the type of flower that will grow underneath the tree.

MOUNTAIN LAUREL

JACK-IN-THE-PULPIT

BIRD'S-FOOT VIOLET

CYNTHIA

The joy of spring!

DOGTOOTH VIOLET

BUNCHBERRY

BELLWORT
PAINTED
TRILLIUM
DUTCHMAN'S
BREECHES
GOAT'S-RUE
SESSILE-FLOWERED TRILLIUM
SHOWY LADY-SLIPPER
PINXTER
JACOB'S LADDER
WILD GERANIUM
HEPATICA
MAY APPLE
WHORLED POGONIA
WILD GINGER
FALSE SOLOMON'S-SEAL
HAWKWEED
EARLY MEADOW-RUE
FALSE FOXGLOVE

Some wild flowers are very easily grown from seeds. Seeds can be bought from seed companies that specialize in wild flowers, or gathered from wild plants. Seeds are ripe and ready to be gathered when the fruit that contains them splits or becomes dry and brown. Each kind of seed needs a certain temperature in order to grow. Some plants have seeds that sprout during the summer when the weather is warm. Many plants that grow where the winters are cold have seeds that will not begin to sprout unless they are kept cold for a while. Such seeds are either planted outside in the fall or put in damp sand or soil in a covered jar and kept in a refrigerator for a month or two. If you buy seeds, the company that sells them will be glad to tell you how and when to plant each kind. If you gather the seeds yourself, from plants that grow in your climate, just plant them outside right away.

Why are climate and temperature important to seeds?

Mark the spot where you plant the seeds and keep them watered. If they do not sprout during warm weather, perhaps they will sprout during the cool autumn period. Or perhaps they need the winter frosts to make them sprout the following spring. Wait and see, and do not disturb them.

How should seeds be planted?

Seeds should be planted three times as deep as the thickness of that particular kind of seed. The soil that covers them should have no lumps or pebbles in it. If you can, sift the soil through a piece of wire

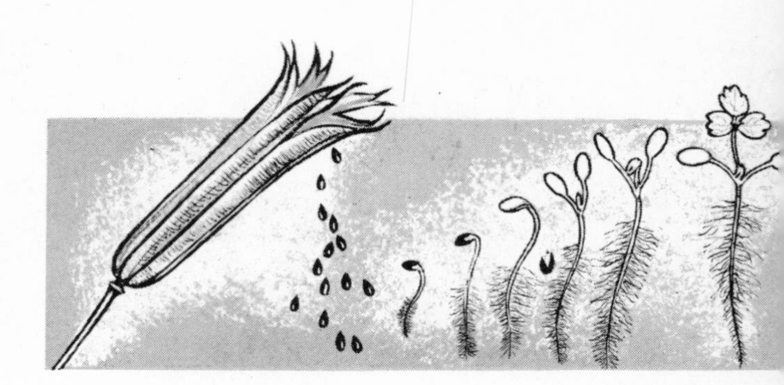

mesh or screening before covering the seeds with it. Very tiny seeds should be scattered on top of the smoothed or sifted soil, with just a little very fine soil sifted over them until they are barely covered.

Plant the seeds in a special seed bed or in clay flowerpots. The soil of the seed bed should be dug up and raked smooth. If it is very sandy, or if it seems to be mostly clay, mix some peat moss or sifted leafmold into it. You can buy peat moss, or dig up some leafmold from beneath the trees in a forest. If you are using flowerpots, it is also good to use peat moss or leafmold. Use about one potful of it to every three pots of soil.

How can you guard against plant dryness, mold and mildew?

When you wish to store seeds, keep them dry. When you wish them to grow, keep them damp. Once a seed begins to sprout, it may die if it dries out too much. So be sure that your seed bed or flowerpots are always damp. Flowerpots are convenient to use because they can be moved around without disturbing the seeds, but they are apt to dry out. If you bury the pots up to their rims in the soil of the garden, there will be less danger of their drying out quickly. Do not keep the seed bed or pots *too* wet,

This shows the development of a wild colombine from seed to flowering plant. The two cotyledons that emerge from the seed help to nourish the small plant until it grows leaves to make its own food.

or they will get moldy. Try to grow your seeds in a place that is protected from too much sun or wind, which will dry them out quickly. If there is any danger, cover the pots with a layer of straw, or burlap, or evergreen branches or anything else that is suitable. If you have planted the seeds inside your house, it might be good to cover the pots with a pane of glass. Prop the glass up on one or both sides with a strip of wood or thick cardboard, or push the pane aside a little, so that air can circulate in and out. Otherwise there is danger from molds and mildew. If the sun is strong, shade the pots with a piece of paper.

Plant only one kind of seed in a pot and label it carefully. If two kinds of seeds are planted together, they may come up at different times and need different amounts of sun and water.

Where can you plant seeds?

Seeds can be planted in wooden boxes as well as in pots. A box will leak, however, and must be put outside or in a place where it will not harm anything. If the box *does not* leak, that isn't any good, either. All boxes and pots must have holes or cracks from which extra water can drain, or else there is a good chance that the soil will get too wet. If the holes are so big that the soil comes out as well as the water, cover the holes with pieces of broken flowerpots.

Which common flowers are easy to grow?

Try growing some of the common field and roadside flowers from seed. They are often grown more quickly and easily than woodland flowers, and many of them make beautiful garden plants. Some of the best are buttercup, daisy, black-eyed Susan, wild geranium, orange milkweed and goldenrod.

Many people think that the pollen of goldenrod causes hay fever, but this is not so. It is the ragweed pollen, in bloom at the same time as goldenrod, that is blown about by the wind and can be breathed in with the air to cause hay fever. Goldenrod pollen is too heavy to float in the air, and it is carried from one blossom to another by bees. It never reaches our noses.

Among the woodland flowers, columbine and the many kinds of anemones and violets are rather easy to grow.

FLOWERS OF THE FIELD

Most of the 120,000 known species of flowering plants grow in prairies, plains and open lowlands. They are in blossom every month of the year in some part of the world. The North American prairies are a treasure chest of wild flowers in the spring and early summer, while the field and wayside plants of the East are more eye-catching in the fall. The grass family is, by far, the most important family of food plants to man and animal. The members of the goldenrod family are found mostly in the eastern part of the United States and are often a cause of irritation to hayfever sufferers. The many species of milkweed can be found all over the United States. They bloom in the summer and fall, and their seed parachutes are a familiar sight. The joe-pye weed belongs to the composites, and it is widely distributed in the eastern United States. Most species of lupines are confined to the western part of the United States. They belong to the pea family and bloom in the spring and early summer. The butter-and-eggs, a member of the figwort family, came originally from Europe, and have spread over the northern United States. They bloom in late summer and early fall. Chicory, another European plant that abounds in the United States, is used as a coffee substitute. The roots of the plant are ground and roasted. Most of the asters adorn the fields in the eastern United States in late fall. In America, there are about sixty species of sunflowers, of which about forty species grow east of the Rockies. One species, the Jerusalem artichoke, has edible tubers and is grown as a crop plant. The thistles, which crowd fields, roadsides and pastures, are spring and early summer flowers. Goldfinches use thistledown to line their nests.

STEEPLEBUSH
IRONWEED
CARDINAL
FLOWER
SPIDERWORT
BLADDER
CHAMPION
BINDWEED
VETCH
FIELD DAISY
THISTLE
RED CLOVER

A *perennial* plant is one that lives from year to year. Some last for only a few years, others for many years. *Annual* plants, such as touch-me-not and yellow wood sorrel, grow each year from seed formed the year before, and then die. Perennial plants usually do not flower until they are one or more years old. Annuals bloom the same year they are planted, which is the only year that they are alive.

Annuals, perennials, biennials: What are the differences?

Some plants, such as the black-eyed Susan, Queen Anne's lace and evening primrose are called *biennial*. When biennial seeds are planted, they grow during the warm season, rest over the winter and flower during the next year. Then they die, and the seeds that they have formed will bloom the second year after *they* are planted.

It is important to know whether a wild flower you want to grow is annual or perennial. If it is perennial, you will know that even though it looks brown and dead during the winter, it will grow again the next spring. Therefore, it should not be pulled up and thrown away. If it is annual, you must make sure that some of its seeds are left undisturbed in the soil over the winter or saved in an envelope. They can then be planted in the spring.

Where winters are cold, some perennial plants from southern climates die unless they are dug up and brought indoors. Their seeds, however, might be able to live through freezing weather and sprout in the spring. In northern climates, such perennial plants can be grown as if they were annuals. Petunias and snapdragons are examples of this. True annuals, such as zinnias, do not live more than a year even when they are grown in a southern climate.

Many wild flowers are perennial. Some of them, like partridgeberry and mountain laurel, keep their leaves and stems alive all year. Others die down during certain seasons of the year, but the underground parts remain alive and send up new stems, leaves and flowers year after year.

What is transplanting?

If you are able to find wild flower plants that are common enough so that the Wildflower Preservation Society does not ask us to protect them, you can dig them up and plant them again in your garden. This process of moving a plant from the spot where it is growing to another place is called

transplanting. If you find a place that is about to be built upon, it is good to take all the plants you can grow, since otherwise they will all die.

How and when are plants transplanted?

Young plants are easier to transplant than older plants. It is also usually better to move a plant that is not flowering at the time. In most cases, the best thing to do is to transplant young plants very early in the spring when they first begin to grow after their winter's rest. Dig them out with their roots undisturbed in a clump of earth as big as you can manage. Some wild flowers have roots that spread out close to the soil surface, while others have roots that are deep down. Unless you know just how your plant grows, dig deep down at a good distance all around the plant to be sure of getting all the roots. Place the clump of earth in your garden exactly as it was in the wild, neither deeper in the ground nor shallower. Plant it in the same type of place in which you found it growing — sunny or shady, and in a similar type of soil. You can add builder's sand, or leafmold or both, if it seems needed. Press the garden soil gently but firmly around the clump of earth and water it thoroughly.

How should you care for transplanted wild flowers?

All newly transplanted wild flowers will need a lot of attention at first. Don't let the soil get dry. It may need water several times a day. It will help if you shade the plant with a newspaper for several days. Plants get enough light for food-making right through the paper. Put the paper over the plants like a two-sided tent, and pin down the edges with sticks or rocks. If you transplant wild flowers carefully, they will stay fresh and not wilt, and they will soon begin to grow again. In a successful garden the plants will thrive as well as they do in the wild.

Things to Do With Wild Flowers

How can wild flowers be pressed?

Perhaps you would like to preserve some wild flowers by pressing them. Pressing makes them flat and dry so that they can be arranged and pasted on paper.

Pressing wild flowers and making a herbarium is instructive and entertaining. But you will also want to study living plants.

Flowers that are pressed correctly keep their colors for a long time. To do a good job, the most important thing to remember is that pressed plants must be dried quickly and thoroughly. Thick juicy plants will be much harder to press than thin ones.

You will need two smooth flat boards, several pieces of corrugated cardboard, newspaper and plenty of large blotters such as are used on desks. All these things should be cut to the same size, except the newspaper, which should be the same size only *after* it is folded in half. A convenient size is one and a half to two feet square.

Put a piece of corrugated cardboard on one of the boards and a blotter on top of the cardboard. Put a piece of newspaper on the blotter and arrange a plant between its folds. Try to keep the parts of the plant from overlapping each other. You will find that it is easiest to arrange plants that have wilted just a little bit. Plants that are very fresh and crisp do not bend easily or stay in the position in which you put them. Now put another piece of blotter on the paper, then corrugated cardboard, then another blotter and another plant folded in a sheet of newspaper. Continue in this way, making "sandwiches" of flowers between newspaper and blotters, with the sandwiches separated by corrugated cardboard. The second board goes on top of the whole pile.

Now you must apply pressure to the flowers in order to squeeze out their juice, which will be soaked up by the blotters. One way is to put a strap around each end of the pile. Sit on the pile and pull the straps as tight as you

FLOWERS OF THE MOUNTAINS

ALPINE SHOOTING STARS

Mountain flowers, which grow at high elevations above the timber line, are known as alpine plants. They grow during the warmer months of the year in places where the sun has melted the snow. Blossom time begins in April for some alpine plants, though most of them bloom in July. How soon this occurs is also determined by the geographical location of the plant and the intensity of the sunlight. Alpine plants have a much shorter growing season than other plants, and so they produce seeds very quickly. This rapid growth is also true for the stems and flowers, many of which are shorter or smaller than the same species that grow in the lowlands. Compare the alpine bouncing Bet, for example, with the two-foot-high meadow variety.

BLUE COLUMBINE

can. If you have just a few layers of plants, and the pile is not too high and wobbly, you can put heavy books on the top for pressure instead of the straps. Leave the drying plants alone for about twelve hours, and then open the pile and replace the blotters with fresh ones. You can open the folded newspaper and rearrange the plants a little. Arrange the pile just as it was at first, and strap it up again or put back the heavy books. Spread out the damp blotters and let them dry again. Change the blotters again after a day or two. By this time most plants will be completely dry. If any are not, keep pressing them between dry blotters until they are dry. Keeping the pile in the sun or near a radiator (but not *on* it), will help to dry them quickly.

Pressed plants can be pasted onto pieces of stiff paper. Rubber cement is good to use since it is colorless, and any extra cement that smears onto the paper can be rubbed off easily after it is dry. You might like to make your own greeting cards and decorate them with pressed flowers. Cellophane or tissue paper should be used to cover the flowers. Then you can be sure that they won't arrive crumbled in the bottom of the envelope.

What is a herbarium?

A *herbarium* is a collection of pressed plants kept for scientific purposes. Each plant is mounted on a separate sheet of paper, on which is written the plant's scientific name and where and when it was collected. Herbarium plants are often fastened to the paper with a few thin strips of tape, rather than paste, so that they can be easily removed.

Why is a herbarium useful to scientists?

If a scientist wants to know exactly what a certain plant looks like, the best thing for him to do is to find the plant growing in its natural state. But suppose this particular plant grows only in faraway countries, or suppose the scientist is in a hurry and the plant grows only at a different time of the year. Now, if the scientist can find a good photograph of the plant, he might be able to see what he wants to know about it. But suppose he wants to see exactly how the leaves are attached to the stem or how many stamens are in each flower? Such details do not always show up on a photograph.

In many such cases, the scientist finds the plant he needs in a herbarium. Here he has the actual plant, even though it is pressed and dried. He can take it apart and see exactly what he wants to know. He can look at it with a magnifying glass if necessary.

As you have learned, there are many small variations among plants of any one kind. Sometimes scientists want to find out just how much the leaves of a certain kind of plant can vary in size. There are herbariums that have many pressed plants of each kind. The scientist can look at all of them and measure their leaves. Since every plant is labeled to show where it grew and when it was picked, he might find out that the plants of a certain kind growing in one place usually have larger leaves than those of the same kind growing elsewhere.

If a plant is found by someone who wants to know its name, it can be taken to a herbarium. There it can be compared with the pressed specimens until

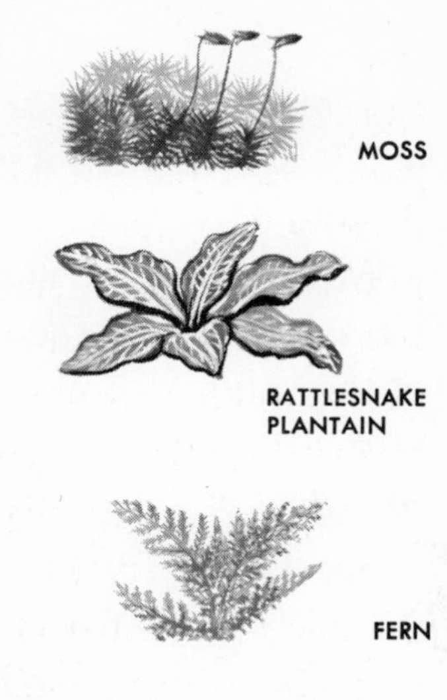

Before building your terrarium, assemble all the materials carefully.

one of the same kind is found. Occasionally, someone sends a plant to a large herbarium to be identified, but no plant of the same kind can be found. The people in charge can send the plant to other herbariums all over the world. If there is no place that has a named specimen of the same kind, it means that a new plant has been discovered.

What is a terrarium?

You probably know what an *aquarium* is. *Aqua* means "water" in Latin, and an aquarium is a glass bowl with water in it. Fish, water snails, water plants and anything else that lives in water can be kept in an aquarium. *Terra* means "land" in Latin, and a *terrarium* is a glass bowl with soil on the bottom. Some kinds of little plants can be grown in a terrarium.

How can you make a terrarium?

You can make a terrarium with wild flowers in a glass bowl or tank. Small plants that grow slowly are best, since bigger ones need too much room. The bottom of the bowl can be filled with potting soil or a mixture of building sand (the kind used with cement to make concrete) and peat moss. If you do not know where to buy potting soil and peat moss, perhaps a florist can tell you. Try arranging the soil or peat moss and sand in different ways. It can be a bit higher in the back of the bowl. The surface does not have to be even, and it will look more attractive if it is a little hilly.

Perhaps you can find a few woodland plants that are common enough to be dug up. Ferns and mosses look particularly attractive in a terrarium even though they have no flowers. It is best to look for young fern plants that are small enough to be easily transplanted. Older plants have bigger roots and you might injure them too much while digging. If the fern grows too big later on in your terrarium, you can cut off the oldest leaves now and then, and perhaps that will keep the plant small enough.

Moss is very difficult to transplant and seldom lives very long afterwards, but look for a nice patch of it growing on a small stone. Take the moss with the stone, or else peel the moss off very carefully and press it gently into the soil in your terrarium.

Many kinds of violets do well in a terrarium. Maianthemum, or false lily of the valley as it is sometimes called, is attractive and common. It might spread too quickly, however, and it isn't evergreen, but it is worth trying. Partridgeberry and wintergreen, tiny plants with evergreen leaves and bright red berries, are excellent. They have stems that creep along the soil in the woods. Neither of these should be disturbed if they grow wild, but they can be bought from a wild flower nursery.

How should you take care of a terrarium?

Be careful not to water a terrarium too much. If you are not sure whether you are watering the terrarium correctly, put your finger down into the soil. It should feel damp, but not wet, and it should not be dry. If you cover the terrarium with a pane of glass, it will stay damp for a long time between waterings and the plants will grow well. If it seems to be too damp inside, leave a small opening at the top or take the glass pane off entirely until the terrarium dries out a bit.

Terrariums usually look best with only a few plants rather than with many plants. Try to make them look like landscapes, with one or two taller plants, a few very short ones and perhaps some small rocks placed among them. For those who enjoy wild flowers, yet live far from the countryside, a thriving terrarium of woodland flowers is a cheerful reminder of where they grow.

One way to display your flowers is in an "eggshell garden." If you color the eggshells first, you will have a symphony of color when your plants begin to bloom.